SIMPLY THE BEST
BLENDER RECIPES

MARIAN GETZ

INTRODUCTION BY WOLFGANG PUCK

Copyright © 2016 Marian Getz

AS I LEARNED LONG AGO, ALONGSI
AND GRANDMOTHER, YOU SHOULD
LOTS OF LOVE INTO EVERYTHING YO
IS CERTAINLY EVIDENT IN THIS COOI

Wolfgang Puck

The modern tools we have in the kitchen, whether in the restaurant or at home, are expected to be able to do more than one thing. While a blender is typically thought of as an appliance that can only make shakes or drinks, it is capable of performing a variety of tasks. The blender is a kitchen tool that can be used to make anything from breakfast to dinner, including hot soups without the use of a stovetop.

Marian's blender cookbook is a wonderful collection of recipes for this appliance. She has taken her experiences as a chef, mother and grandmother to write recipes that will even make a novice cook feel like a pro. Her recipes are easy to follow and taste incredible.

A student of cooking is probably one of the best ways to describe Marian. She is always looking for something new, something fresh, something local, something seasonal. Her culinary knowledge combined with her passion for cooking is second to none. The recipes that Marian has written for this cookbook and the ease of which they can be prepared will motivate you to become more creative in the kitchen.

BLENDER TIPS

Your Wolfgang Puck Blender has the ability to process frozen drinks, crush ice, chop ingredients, knead dough and even heat soup. Below are some tips to help you make the most out of the Blender and this cookbook:

MANUAL MODE VS AUTOMATIC PROGRAMS

Your Blender has 10 variable speeds and 4 automatic programs. The automatic programs include Soup, Smoothie, Ice Crush and Self-Clean. The beauty of these automatic programs is that you can select them and walk away to attend to other tasks while the Blender operates these automatic programs without the need to supervise. If you choose the "Soup" program, you do not necessarily need to wait until the cycle is completed if the soup is hot and steamy prior to the end of the cycle. You can test this by slowly and carefully lifting the Filler Cap. If steam comes out then the contents are hot and you can manually shut off the Blender. You can also place your hand on the outside of the Blender Jar to feel when it is sufficiently hot. The "Smoothie" program can be run more than 1 cycle to achieve the desired result. The 10 variable speeds allow you to manually adjust the Blender to fine-tune the speeds according to the recipe or desired outcome. It is a more precise way of blending however it requires manual operation. When blending manually, watch closely to monitor the progress. The Blender can create enough friction that it quickly heats the ingredients inside. This is fine when making soups or sauces but it is not desirable if you are making smoothies or ice cream. Both methods are used throughout the book and should be followed when making a recipe. For more details about each automatic program, please refer to your Blender manual.

MANUAL MODE SPEED SETTINGS

Manual speed 1-3 are considered "low" speeds, 4-7 are "medium" speeds and 8-10 are "high" speeds. The "pulse" function allows you to briefly pulse the Blender on and off without having to turn the control knob each time. Pulsing is best when you want to roughly chop or incorporate an ingredient without over blending or pureeing.

THICK OR FROZEN INGREDIENTS

For very thick or frozen mixtures, the sound of your Blender will change dramatically during operation. For thick and very dry mixtures such as peanut butter, you will hear a high pitched sound. This is caused by an air pocket being formed around the blade. The high pitched sound is the result of the blades spinning freely without resistance. Use the Tamper to push the ingredients back towards the blades. A low growling sound indicates that the Blender's motor is working harder as the blades come into contact with thicker ingredients. These sounds are normal occurrences and are not a cause for concern as your Blender can easily handle those ingredients. Your Blender also has a feature where it shuts itself off to prevent overheating. If this occurs, please allow the Blender to cool off before blending again.

BLENDING IN BATCHES

Your Blender Jar should not be overfilled with ingredients or you might not be able to blend them properly. If blending a large amount of ingredients, divide them and blend in batches to achieve a superior result.

TAMPER

The Tamper will help you push ingredients towards the blades to fully incorporate them. It is especially helpful when blending thick or dry ingredients. It is designed to not come into contact with the blades so that you can blend while inserting it through the Lid opening. Because the Tamper occupies space inside the Blender Jar, it is best to remove for foods that can blend themselves without the aid of the Tamper.

SAUCES

For emulsified sauces such as mayonnaise, pour the oil or melted butter through the Lid opening while blending. Pour it in a slow and thin stream to avoid the oil pooling on top of the other ingredients. This will ensure that the sauce comes out smooth and creamy. To prevent spattering when adding ingredients, hold a folded kitchen towel to cover most of the Lid opening while adding ingredients or use a funnel.

GREEN SMOOTHIES

When blending smoothies containing both fruits and vegetables, using too many vegetables might result in an undesirable taste. As a general rule, it is best to keep the ratio 60% fruits and 40% vegetables to achieve a balanced smoothie where the fruit flavor dominates over the vegetables. You can adjust the ratio to your liking.

PROTEIN SHAKES

If you are using the Blender to make protein shakes, add all other ingredients first, starting with the liquids, blend until smooth then add the protein powder and pulse until mixed. This helps control excess foaminess.

CLEANING YOUR BLENDER

The Self-Clean program of your Blender makes cleaning a breeze. Fill the Blender half full of water, add a few drops of dish soap and let the Blender clean itself. When the Self-Clean program cycle is complete, simply rinse out the Blender Jar and dry thoroughly. You may run the Self-Clean program multiple times if needed, especially for cleaning oily or sticky ingredients such as peanut butter.

PANTRY TIPS

Being prepared to cook the recipes in this book, or any recipe for that matter, is one of the keys to success in the kitchen. Your pantry must be stocked with the basics. We all know how frustrating it can be when you go to the cupboard and what you need is not there. This list includes some of the ingredients you will find in this book and some that we feel are important to always have on hand.

PERISHABLES	SPICES	DRY GOODS
ONIONS	KOSHER SALT	SUGARS
GARLIC	FRESH PEPPERCORNS	SUGAR SUBSTITUTE
TOMATOES	BAY LEAVES	HONEY AND VANILLA
CARROTS	SAGE	EXTRACTS/FLAVORINGS
CELERY	OREGANO	AGAVE SYRUP
GINGER	THYME	CANNED TOMATOES
BELL PEPPERS	CHILI FLAKES	CANNED BEANS
WHITE POTATOES	CUMIN SEEDS	CANNED VEGETABLES
SWEET POTATOES	CURRY POWDER	DRIED CHILLIES
SQUASHES	ONION POWDER	PASTA
CITRUS	GARLIC POWDER	LENTILS
APPLES	DRY MUSTARD	STOCKS
BANANAS	GROUND CINNAMON	POWDERED BOUILLON
LETTUCE	NUTMEG	OLIVES
SPINACH	CLOVES	KETCHUP
FRESH HERBS	CHILI POWDER	MUSTARD
GREEN ONIONS		PICKLES
MILK		OILS
CREAM CHEESE		VINEGAR
PARMESAN CHEESE		HONEY
YOGURT		
OTHER CHEESES YOU LIKE		
FROZEN FRUIT/VEGETABLES		

It is not necessary to have all the items listed at all times. However, if you are feeling creative, adventurous or just following a recipe, it's great to have a good selection in the kitchen.

9

GREEN SMOOTHIE

Makes 2 servings

Ingredients:

1 cup green grapes

1 wedge pineapple with the core (about 1/8 of a pineapple)

1 orange, mostly peeled

1 lemon, peeled

1 very ripe banana (frozen if desired)

1 kiwi, peeled or unpeeled

2 fresh ginger coins

1 tablespoon flax seeds

3 cups loosely packed spinach

1-2 cups frozen broccoli

Method:

1. *Place all ingredients in the order listed into the Blender Jar; cover with Lid and insert Tamper.*
2. *Blend using the SMOOTHIE PROGRAM (use Tamper as needed).*
3. *When blending is complete, pour into glasses and serve.*

TIP

Green smoothies are a great place to use up leftovers. Berries that are a bit too ripe, leftover peas, carrots or broccoli are all good additions to smoothies and will not affect the taste.

WHOLE FRUIT
MARGARITA

Makes 2 servings

Ingredients:

2 tablespoons sugar
2 ounces tequila
1 lime, peeled + more for salt garnish
1 orange, peeled
1 small red grapefruit, peeled
1 ounce triple sec or orange liqueur
4 cups ice cubes
Salt for rims of glasses

Method:

1. *Place all ingredients, except salt, into the Blender Jar; cover with Lid.*
2. *Blend on SPEED 9-10 for 8 seconds or until smooth.*
3. *Use a piece of lime to moisten the rims of the glasses.*
4. *Dip glass rims in salt until rims are covered.*
5. *Pour margarita into glasses below the salt rim and serve immediately.*

STRAWBERRY
ICE CREAM

Makes 4 servings

Ingredients:

1 pound frozen strawberries
1 cup whole milk
1 cup powdered sugar

Method:

1. *Place all ingredients into the Blender Jar; cover with Lid and insert Tamper.*
2. *Blend on SPEED 9-10, pushing the berries towards the blades using the Tamper until mixture is smooth and thick. Do not over blend or melting will occur from the friction.*
3. *When blending is complete, serve immediately.*

TIP

For strawberry sorbet, omit the milk and use cranberry or apple juice instead.

CREAMY BROCCOLI CHEESE SOUP

Makes 4 servings

Ingredients:

1 bag (14 ounces) frozen broccoli, thawed and divided or leftover cooked broccoli

2 tablespoons unsalted butter

1 small yellow onion, quartered

4 Italian style bread slices

2 cups chicken or vegetable stock

Kosher salt and fresh pepper to taste

1 teaspoon lemon juice

1 teaspoon honey

1/4 cup half & half or milk

1/3 cup Parmesan cheese, grated

1/2 cup shredded Cheddar cheese + more for serving

Method:

1. *Place half of the broccoli and remaining ingredients into the Blender Jar; cover with Lid.*
2. *Blend using the SOUP PROGRAM until hot and steamy.*
3. *When blending is complete, add remaining broccoli and blend on SPEED 1-2 just until broccoli is chunky.*
4. *Pour soup into bowls, top with Cheddar cheese, garnish as desired and serve.*

TIP

Do not use raw or fresh broccoli as the raw taste negatively affects the outcome of this recipe.

SILKY SMOOTH GUACAMOLE

Makes 4-6 servings

Ingredients:

3 ripe avocados, peeled and pitted
1/2 cup ice
Zest of 1 lime
Juice of 2 limes
1/8 medium white onion
A palmful of fresh cilantro
Jalapeño or Serrano chili peppers to taste
Kosher salt to taste

Method:

1. *Place all ingredients into the Blender Jar; cover with Lid and insert Tamper.*
2. *Blend on SPEED 9-10, pushing the ingredients towards the blades using the Tamper.*
3. *Blend for 30 seconds or until completely smooth.*
4. *When blending is complete, serve as desired.*

TIP

To store, press plastic wrap directly against the surface of the guacamole to prevent browning due to the exposure to air.

STEALTH HEALTH SMOOTHIE

Makes 2 servings

Ingredients:

1 bag (16 ounces) frozen kale, collard or turnip greens, thawed

1 very ripe banana (frozen if desired)

1 orange, peeled

1 lemon, peeled

A few fresh ginger coins to taste

Pinch of turmeric powder

1/2 teaspoon ground cinnamon

1 tablespoon each flax seeds, goji berries and hemp seeds

3 cups carrot juice

2 cups frozen blueberries or mixed berries

Method:

1. *Place all ingredients, except berries, into the Blender Jar; cover with Lid.*

2. *Blend using the SMOOTHIE PROGRAM.*

3. *When blending is complete, add the berries, cover with Lid and blend on SPEED 9-10 for a few seconds to liquefy the berries (the color will change from green to a muddy brown).*

4. *Pour into glasses and serve.*

TIP

Add some of the zest from the citrus for an even more fruity flavor.

MODERN
MAC & CHEESE

Makes 4 servings

Ingredients:

6 ounces extra-sharp Cheddar cheese, cubed
2 ounces Parmesan cheese, cubed
1 1/2 cups whole milk
3 tablespoons unsalted butter
3 Italian style bread slices
1 medium carrot, peeled
1 teaspoon kosher salt
Pinch of cayenne pepper
1/2 teaspoon dry mustard powder
6 cups elbow macaroni, cooked and hot

Method:

1. *Place all ingredients, except macaroni, into the Blender Jar; cover with Lid.*
2. *Blend using the SOUP PROGRAM until hot and steamy.*
3. *Place macaroni in large mixing bowl.*
4. *Pour cheese mixture over macaroni and stir to combine.*
5. *Garnish as desired and serve.*

HOMEMADE PEANUT BUTTER

Makes about 1 cup

Ingredients:

3 cups roasted peanuts

Method:

1. *Place peanuts into the Blender Jar; cover with Lid and insert Tamper.*
2. *Blend on SPEED 9-10, pushing the peanuts towards the blades using the Tamper until blender changes to a growling sound (about 2-3 minutes).*
3. *Transfer peanut butter to an airtight container.*
4. *Store at room temperature and use within 1 week.*
5. *Natural oil from the peanuts will rise to the top as it stands. Stir the oil back into the peanut butter instead of pouring it out to prevent it from becoming stiff and dry in texture.*

TIP

You can use this same technique with other nuts to make nut butters. Toasted cashews, hazelnuts, pecans, macadamia nuts and almonds are a wonderful alternative. For some of these drier nuts, add some canola oil or water while blending. You can also add a handful of chocolate chips and make a delicious chocolate-flavored nut butter.

NO CHURN
ICE CREAM

Makes 4 servings

Ingredients:

2 cups heavy cream
1 can (14 ounces) sweetened condensed milk
1 teaspoon vanilla extract
2 teaspoons or 1 packet instant coffee powder (optional)
1/2 cup toasted hazelnuts, crushed (optional)

Method:

1. *Place the cream into the Blender Jar; cover with Lid.*
2. *Blend on SPEED 5-6 for 15 seconds or until thickened (do not over blend).*
3. *Add the condensed milk and vanilla then cover with Lid and blend on SPEED 1-2 just to incorporate.*
4. *Scrape cream mixture into a plastic wrap-lined container then smooth the top.*
5. *Sprinkle surface with coffee powder and hazelnuts if desired.*
6. *Cover pan with plastic wrap and freeze for a minimum of 4 hours or up to 2 days.*
7. *Serve as desired.*

TIP

This delicious vanilla ice cream goes well with any flavor topping. If you prefer to omit the coffee and hazelnuts from the recipe, you can use your favorite add-in such as chocolate-filled cookies, strawberries, gummy bears or marshmallows.

CARROT SOUP

Makes 4 servings

Ingredients:

1 tablespoon unsalted butter

1/3 small yellow onion

8 carrots (about 1 pound), peeled

2 fresh ginger coins

1 tablespoon honey

Kosher salt and fresh pepper to taste

1 1/2 cups chicken or vegetable stock

A few sprigs fresh dill + more for serving

Method:

1. *Place all ingredients into the Blender Jar; cover with Lid.*
2. *Blend using the SOUP PROGRAM until hot and steamy.*
3. *Ladle into soup bowls and garnish with additional dill.*

TIP

For a creamier version, add 1/4 cup unsalted butter towards the end of the blending cycle.

RANCH
DIP

Makes 2 cups

Ingredients:

1 cup sour cream
1 cup mayonnaise
1/2 cup buttermilk
1 tablespoon apple cider vinegar
3 garlic cloves
Kosher salt and fresh pepper to taste
1/2 cup loosely packed mixture of basil leaves, parsley, green onions, tarragon and dill

Method:

1. *Place all ingredients, except herb mixture, into the Blender Jar; cover with Lid.*
2. *Blend on SPEED 5-6 until combined.*
3. *Add the herb mixture, replace Lid and blend on SPEED 1-2 until herb pieces are small but still visible.*
4. *When blending is complete, transfer to a storage container.*
5. *Keep refrigerated for up to 1 week.*

TIP

To turn this dip into a dressing simply increase the buttermilk to 1 cup.

VEGETABLE BASED BABY FOOD

Makes about 3/4 cup

Ingredients:

Peas:
1 cup frozen peas, thawed
1/3 cup water

Carrots:
3 medium carrots, trimmed and peeled
1/2 cup water
(cut carrots into 1-inch sections then steam until tender prior to blending)

Potatoes:
2 medium potatoes, peeled
2/3 cup water
(cut potatoes into 1-inch sections then steam until tender prior to blending)

Beets:
3 medium fresh beets, peeled
1/4 cup water
(cut beets into 1-inch sections then steam until tender prior to blending)

Method:

1. *Place desired vegetables and water into the Blender Jar; cover with Lid.*
2. *Blend on SPEED 9-10 until smooth, scraping down the Blender Jar as needed.*
3. *If desired, pour mixture through a fine mesh strainer for a smoother consistency.*
4. *Serve within 2 days or freeze in individual portions for later use.*

TIP

The easiest way to steam vegetables is in the steamer basket of the Wolfgang Puck rice cooker or electric steamer. Add about 2 inches of water to the rice cooker insert, place the foods to be steamed into the steamer basket and let it steam. Start checking for doneness after about 5 minutes of steaming.

CREAM OF TOMATO SOUP

Makes 4 servings

Ingredients:

1/2 small yellow onion
1/2 celery stalk
1/2 small carrot, peeled
1 garlic clove
1 tablespoon honey
Kosher salt and fresh pepper to taste
Pinch of baking soda
Pinch of dried thyme
1 tablespoon unsalted butter
2 Italian style bread slices
1 can (14.5 ounces) stewed tomatoes (or 4 large ripe tomatoes)
1/4 cup heavy cream or milk

Method:

1. *Place all ingredients into the Blender Jar; cover with Lid.*
2. *Blend using the SOUP PROGRAM until hot and steamy.*
3. *When blending is complete, pour into bowls, garnish as desired and serve.*

WOLF'S BLUEBERRY
ICE CREAM

Makes 4 servings

Ingredients:

1 pound wild, organic frozen blueberries
1 cup powdered sugar or sweetener of your choice
1 cup whole milk

Method:

1. *Place all ingredients into the Blender Jar; cover with Lid and insert the Tamper.*
2. *Blend on SPEED 9-10, pushing the blueberries towards the blades using the Tamper until mixture is smooth and thick. Do not over blend or melting will occur from the friction.*
3. *When blending is complete, serve immediately.*

ORGANIC
POPSICLES

Makes 6 pops

Ingredients:

1 bag (12 ounces) frozen organic peaches, thawed
A small squirt of agave nectar or honey (optional)
Juice from 1/2 lime

Method:

1. *Place all ingredients into the Blender Jar; cover with Lid.*
2. *Blend on SPEED 9-10 for 10 seconds or until smooth.*
3. *Pour mixture into Popsicle molds or small paper cups. If using paper cups, insert a Popsicle stick into the center of each cup then place in the freezer.*
4. *Freeze until solid before serving.*
5. *To easily remove the molds or paper cups, run briefly under cold water.*

RECIPES

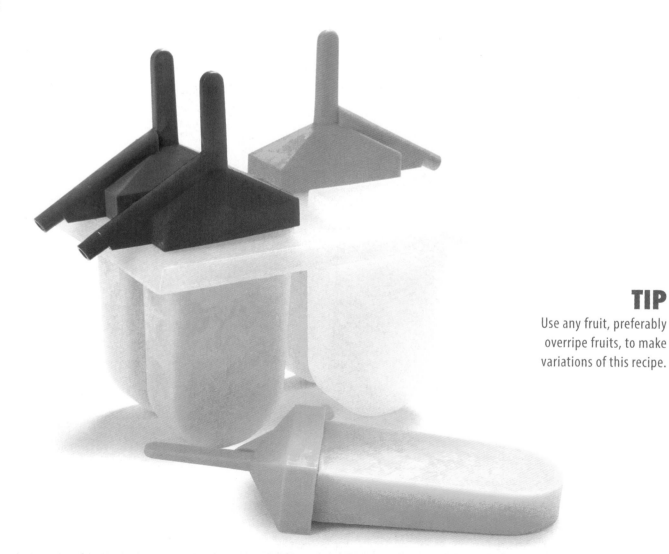

TIP
Use any fruit, preferably overripe fruits, to make variations of this recipe.

CHICKEN TORTILLA SOUP

Makes 2-4 servings

Ingredients:

1 cup chicken stock

1 can (11 ounces) enchilada sauce

Kosher salt and fresh pepper to taste

1/2 cup grape tomatoes

1 cup corn tortilla chips + more for serving

Pinch of ground cumin

A small handful of cilantro

2 cups leftover cooked chicken

1 cup Monterrey Jack cheese, shredded, for serving

1 jalapeño pepper, sliced, for serving

Sour cream, for serving

1 lime, thinly sliced, for serving

Method:

1. *Place stock, enchilada sauce, salt, pepper, tomatoes, tortilla chips, cumin and cilantro into the Blender Jar; cover with Lid.*
2. *Blend using the SOUP PROGRAM until hot and steamy.*
3. *When blending is complete, add the leftover chicken through the Lid opening and blend on SPEED 1-2 until chicken is chunky.*
4. *Pour into bowls and serve topped with additional tortilla chips, cheese, jalapeño peppers, sour cream and lime.*

BEST MOJITO

Makes 2 servings

Ingredients:

Zest and juice from 2 limes

A small handful of fresh mint leaves

2 tablespoons superfine sugar or powdered sugar

2 ounces white rum or to taste

2 cups ice cubes

Method:

1. *Place all ingredients into the Blender Jar; cover with Lid.*
2. *Blend on SPEED 9-10 just until combined and mint pieces are small.*
3. *Pour into glasses and serve over additional ice if desired.*

TIP

For a mango mojito, add
1 cup cubed mango to
the blender.

BUTTER PECAN
MILKSHAKE

Makes 2 servings

Ingredients:

4 scoops vanilla ice cream
1/4 teaspoon vanilla extract
1/4 teaspoon maple extract
1/8 teaspoon butter extract
1/2 cup whole milk
1/2 cup chopped pecans, toasted and divided

Method:

1. *Place all ingredients, except pecans, into the Blender Jar; cover with Lid.*
2. *Blend on SPEED 9-10 for 20 seconds or until smooth (use Tamper as needed).*
3. *Pour 1/4 cup pecans through the Lid opening and PULSE until pecans are chopped into small pieces.*
4. *Place 1 tablespoon of pecans into the bottom of 2 glasses.*
5. *Pour the shake into glasses then sprinkle the top of each shake with remaining pecans.*
6. *Serve immediately.*

CHOCOLATE CRÈME BRÛLÉE

Makes 4-6 servings

Ingredients:

10 large egg yolks
1/2 cup granulated sugar
2 1/4 cups heavy cream
Seeds from 1 vanilla bean
3 ounces bittersweet chocolate
Additional granulated sugar and a blowtorch, for serving

Method:

1. *Place all ingredients, except sugar for serving, into the Blender Jar; cover with Lid.*

2. *Blend on SPEED 9-10 for 5-6 minutes while monitoring the temperature using an instant read thermometer through the Lid opening until temperature reaches 180°F (do not touch the blades with the thermometer).*

3. *Immediately pour mixture into 4-6 small ramekins, filling each to the top.*

4. *Tap ramekins to smooth mixture then refrigerate, uncovered for 1 hour (if storing for longer than 1 hour, cover ramekins).*

5. *To serve, sprinkle an even layer of granulated sugar over the top of each ramekin then use a blowtorch to melt and caramelize the sugar.*

6. *Let stand for a few minutes to allow sugar crust to harden and serve.*

TIP

To make vanilla crème brûlée, simply omit the chocolate. For ginger crème brûlée, omit the chocolate and add 3-5 slices fresh ginger.

EASY

CHEESECAKE

Makes one 8-inch pie

Ingredients:

2 pounds cream cheese, softened
1 cup granulated sugar
6 large eggs
1 store-bought cookie pie crust

Method:

1. *Preheat oven to 350°F and place rack in the center position.*
2. *Place the cream cheese, sugar and eggs into the Blender Jar; cover with Lid and insert Tamper.*
3. *Blend on SPEED 9-10 for 10 seconds or until just liquefied, pushing the cream cheese towards the blades using the Tamper.*
4. *Pour mixture into the pie crust then place in the oven.*
5. *Bake for 30-40 minutes or until puffed and brown on top.*
6. *Remove and serve hot or warm.*

TIP

To make vanilla cheesecake, before blending add 2 teaspoons vanilla extract or to make chocolate cheesecake, add 1/3 cup dark cocoa powder. Depending on the size of your crust, you might have extra batter.

VEGAN
MAYO

Makes 2 1/4 cups

Ingredients:

3/4 cup almond milk

1 1/4 teaspoons xanthan gum (found at most health food stores), measured carefully

1/3 cup apple cider vinegar

1 tablespoon dry mustard powder

2 tablespoons brown grainy mustard

1 tablespoon kosher salt or to taste

1 small date or 1 teaspoon granulated sugar

1 small garlic clove

2 teaspoons onion powder

1 3/4 cups grapeseed or neutral-flavored oil

Method:

1. *Place the almond milk into the Blender Jar; cover with Lid and remove the Filler Cap.*
2. *Cover the Lid opening with a towel to prevent spatter then blend on SPEED 5-6 while adding the xanthan gum to thicken the mixture.*
3. *Blend for 5 seconds then stop and scrape down the Blender Jar.*
4. *Cover with Lid then blend for an additional 5 seconds.*
5. *Add remaining ingredients, except oil, cover then blend again on SPEED 9-10 for 5 seconds.*
6. *Reduce Blender to SPEED 5-6 then pour the oil through the Lid opening in a thin stream (mixture will get lighter and thicker) until all is incorporated.*
7. *When blending is complete, transfer mixture to a canning jar or other storage container until ready to use.*
8. *Keep refrigerated for 3-4 weeks.*

RED
SMOOTHIE

Makes 2 servings

Ingredients:

2 cups red grapes
1 fresh pineapple wedge
1 red apple, quartered
1/8 of a fresh beet
1 orange, peeled
1 banana (frozen if desired)
2 cups frozen strawberries

Method:

1. *Place all ingredients in the order listed into the Blender Jar; cover with Lid and insert Tamper.*
2. *Blend using the SMOOTHIE PROGRAM, pushing the ingredients towards the blades using the Tamper.*
3. *When blending is complete, pour into glasses, garnish as desired and serve.*

STRAWBERRY DAIQUIRI

Makes 2 servings

Ingredients:

3 cups strawberries
2 ounces light rum
1/4 cup powdered sugar
Zest and juice from 1 lemon
3 cups ice cubes

Method:

1. *Place all ingredients into the Blender Jar; cover with Lid and insert Tamper.*
2. *Blend using the SMOOTHIE PROGRAM, pushing the ingredients towards the blades using the Tamper until smooth.*
3. *When blending is complete, pour into glasses and serve immediately.*

TIP

To change this recipe to a blackberry daiquiri, substitute the strawberries with blackberries and increase the powdered sugar to 1/2 cup.

WOLF'S FAVORITE
MANGO SORBET

Makes about 1 quart

Ingredients:

1 pound frozen mango chunks

2 tablespoons granulated sugar or sweetener (optional)

Juice and Zest from 1 lime (optional)

1 cup carrot or mango juice + more if needed

Method:

1. *Place all ingredients into the Blender Jar; cover with Lid and insert Tamper.*
2. *Blend on SPEED 9-10, pushing the mango chunks towards the blades using the Tamper until mixture is smooth and thick. If sorbet is too thick, add additional juice until desired consistency is achieved. Do not over blend or melting will occur from the friction.*
3. *When blending is complete, serve immediately.*

TIP

You can use this recipe as a template to make many other flavor sorbets. Just use frozen fruits and a fruit juice that is the same or complimentary to the fruit.

MODERN SCRAMBLED EGGS

Makes 2 servings

Ingredients:

4 large eggs
2 tablespoons milk
1 tablespoon unsalted butter
Kosher salt and fresh pepper to taste

Method:

1. *Place all ingredients into the Blender Jar; cover with Lid.*
2. *Blend on SPEED 9-10 and watch carefully as you blend. Once the eggs begin to get cooked by the blender's high speed after about 4 minutes, the liquid will suddenly solidify.*
3. *Invert blender and tap sharply to remove the eggs. Do so immediately to avoid overcooking the eggs.*
4. *Adjust seasoning if desired and serve.*

TIP

You can use egg whites only, just be
sure to add enough to barely cover
the top of the blender blades.

STRAWBERRY FREEZER JAM

Makes 4 cups

Ingredients:

4 cups fresh strawberries
1/4 cup fresh lemon juice
4 cups granulated sugar
1 pouch (3 ounces) liquid pectin

Method:

1. *Place the strawberries, lemon juice and sugar into the Blender Jar; cover with Lid.*
2. *PULSE to break up the strawberries a bit then let stand for 15 minutes.*
3. *PULSE 3-4 times then let stand for an additional 15 minutes.*
4. *Add pectin to the Blender Jar and briefly PULSE just to combine the pectin.*
5. *Pour immediately into storage containers then refrigerate for up to 3 months or freeze for up to 1 year.*

CHOCOLATE CHIP MILKSHAKE

Makes 2 servings

Ingredients:

4 scoops vanilla ice cream
1/2 cup whole milk
1/2 teaspoon vanilla extract
1/4 cup milk chocolate chips
4 tablespoons chocolate syrup

Method:

1. *Place ice cream, milk and vanilla into the Blender Jar; cover with Lid.*
2. *Blend on SPEED 9-10 for 20 seconds or until smooth (use Tamper as needed); add milk if desired.*
3. *Add the chocolate chips and PULSE until chips are chopped into small pieces.*
4. *Pour the chocolate syrup into the bottom of two glasses.*
5. *Pour the shake over the syrup into the glasses, top with additional syrup and serve.*

TIP
Choose a quality, strong-flavored chocolate to achieve the best taste.

PEPPERONI PIZZA FONDUE

Makes 3-4 cups

Ingredients:

1/3 cup chicken stock

2 cups jarred pasta sauce

1/2 cup pepperoni slices

1/2 cup Parmesan cheese, cubed

2 cups fresh mozzarella cheese, cubed

4 Italian style bread slices

1/4 cup sun-dried tomatoes in oil, drained

4 garlic cloves

1 small yellow onion, quartered

1/4 red bell pepper

1/3 cup tomato paste

2 teaspoons Italian seasoning

French bread or pretzel rods, for dipping

Method:

1. *Place all ingredients, except bread or rods for serving, into the Blender Jar; cover with Lid.*
2. *Blend using the SOUP PROGRAM until hot and steamy.*
3. *When blending is complete, pour into a serving dish and serve hot with bread or pretzels for dipping.*

TIP

Change this recipe by swapping out ingredients just the way you would build your favorite pizza.

PEANUT BUTTER & JELLY DIP

Makes 2 cups

Ingredients:

1 cup smooth or chunky peanut butter (or use the Homemade Peanut Butter on page 17)
1/2 cup strawberry or other jam (or use the Strawberry Freezer Jam on page 36)
1/2 cup marshmallow fluff
1/2 cup fresh strawberries
Cookies or fruits, for dipping

Method:

1. *Place all ingredients, except strawberries and dippers, into the Blender Jar; cover with Lid.*
2. *Blend on SPEED 9-10 for about 20 seconds or until smooth.*
3. *Add the strawberries, replace Lid then blend on SPEED 1-2 to incorporate strawberries until chunky in texture.*
4. *Pour into a container and serve with dippers.*

EASY BATTER
BREAD

Makes one 10-inch bread

Ingredients:

2 cups water

1 tablespoon (or 1 envelope) yeast

3 tablespoons olive oil + plus more for the sheet pan

1 tablespoon honey

1 tablespoon kosher salt + more for sprinkling

3 cups bleached all purpose flour

1/2 teaspoon fresh thyme leaves

1 green onion, thinly sliced

Fresh black pepper to taste

Method:

1. *Combine the water, yeast, 3 tablespoons oil and honey in the Blender Jar; cover with Lid.*
2. *Blend on SPEED 1-2 for 5 seconds then remove Lid.*
3. *Add the salt and flour; cover with Lid and insert the Tamper.*
4. *Blend on SPEED 1-2, pushing the flour into the dough using the Tamper.*
5. *Stop blender, scrape down the sides of the Blender Jar then blend again on SPEED 1-2 for an additional 5-10 seconds.*
6. *Scrape dough onto an oiled sheet pan then oil the top of the dough as well.*
7. *Let stand for 30 minutes.*
8. *Preheat oven to 450°F.*
9. *Shape dough into a rough 10-inch circle then dimple the top using your fingertips.*
10. *Sprinkle dough with salt, thyme, green onions and pepper.*
11. *Place in oven and bake for 20-25 minutes or until risen and well browned.*
12. *When baking is complete, remove, let stand for 10 minutes to allow bread to firm up and excess moisture to dissipate then serve.*

NO OIL AVOCADO
DIP

Makes 2 cups

Ingredients:

3 ripe avocados, peeled and pitted

2 garlic cloves

A few fresh basil leaves

Zest and juice from 1 lemon

Kosher salt and fresh pepper to taste

1/2 cup grated Parmesan cheese

Crackers or French bread for serving

Method:

1. *Place all ingredients, except crackers or bread, into the Blender Jar; cover with Lid.*
2. *Blend on SPEED 5-6 until well combined.*
3. *Spoon into a dish then top with additional pepper.*
4. *Garnish as desired then serve with crackers or French bread.*

WOLF'S BLENDER GRAVY

When cooking turkey, Wolfgang likes to place some sweet potatoes under the turkey in the roasting pan and use these cooked potatoes as well as some turkey drippings to make a delicious gravy in the blender.

Makes 6 servings

Ingredients:

1 1/4 cups roasted sweet potatoes from under a roast turkey, hot
1 1/4 cups drippings and juices from the roast turkey
1/3 cup unsalted butter
Kosher salt and fresh pepper to taste

Method:

1. *Place all ingredients into the Blender Jar; cover with Lid.*
2. *Blend using the SOUP PROGRAM until hot and steamy.*
3. *When blending is complete, serve hot.*

BLENDER
HOT CHOCOLATE

Makes 2 servings

Ingredients:

2 cups milk

1 cup half & half

1/4 cup granulated sugar

2 teaspoons vanilla extract

4 thin chocolate bars (1.45 ounces each) + more for serving

1 cup mini marshmallows + more for serving

Method:

1. *Place all ingredients into the Blender Jar; cover with Lid.*
2. *Blend using the SOUP PROGRAM until hot and steamy.*
3. *When blending is complete, pour into cups then top with additional marshmallows and chocolate bars before serving.*

OATMEAL BREAKFAST
SMOOTHIE

Makes 2 servings

Ingredients:

1/2 cup rolled oats
1 ripe banana
1 tablespoon flax seeds
1/4 cup dark raisins
1/2 teaspoon ground cinnamon
1 1/2 cups cold almond or regular milk
1 cup ice cubes

Method:

1. *Place all ingredients into the Blender Jar; cover with Lid.*
2. *Blend using the SMOOTHIE PROGRAM.*
3. *When blending is complete, pour into glasses, garnish as desired and serve.*

CREAMY JAPANESE DIPPING SAUCE

Makes 1 1/2 cups

Ingredients:

1/4 cup rice wine vinegar

2 teaspoons wasabi powder or from a tube

1 tablespoon dark sesame oil

2 tablespoons soy sauce

3 tablespoons granulated sugar

1 tablespoon light miso paste

1 cup mayonnaise

1/4 cup heavy cream

Method:

1. *Place all ingredients into the Blender Jar; cover with Lid.*
2. *Blend on SPEED 3-4 for 10 seconds.*
3. *Scrape down the sides of the Blender Jar, cover and blend for an additional 10 seconds.*
4. *Transfer to a storage container and use as desired.*
5. *Keep refrigerated for up to 1 week.*

TIP

Light miso paste is made from fermented soy bean and can be found at most health food stores.

INSTANT
PASTA SAUCE

Makes 3 1/2 cups

Ingredients:

2 cups grape tomatoes
3 garlic cloves
4 big tomatoes, quartered
1 green onion, cut into 1-inch pieces
1 carrot, peeled
1/4 yellow onion
1 can (4 ounces) tomato paste
1 tablespoon paprika
1 teaspoon Italian seasoning
2 tablespoons extra-virgin olive oil
Kosher salt and fresh pepper to taste

Method:

1. *Place all ingredients into the Blender Jar; cover with Lid.*
2. *Blend using the SOUP PROGRAM until hot and steamy.*
3. *Serve over your favorite pasta or use as desired.*

TIP

This sauce will appear more pink than red when just made because the blender incorporates air. The sauce will turn red as its air bubbles dissipate.

GREEN PEA HUMMUS

Makes 2 cups

Ingredients:

1 bag (12 ounces) peas, thawed (reserve some peas for topping)
1/4 cup almond or regular milk
3 Medjool dates or 2 tablespoons granulated sugar
1/3 cup extra-virgin olive oil + more for serving
Zest and juice from 1 lemon
3 green onions, coarsely chopped
A handful of fresh mint
A few fresh basil leaves
Leaves from 1 thyme sprig
Kosher salt and fresh pepper to taste
Pinch of truffle salt (optional)
Dippers of your choice

Method:

1. *Place all ingredients, except dippers, into the Blender Jar; cover with Lid.*
2. *Blend on SPEED 9-10 for 10 seconds.*
3. *Scrape down the Blender Jar, adjust thickness with oil or milk if desired then cover with Lid and blend for an additional 10 seconds or until smooth.*
4. *Transfer to a serving plate and top with reserved peas.*
5. *Drizzle with additional oil, salt and pepper then garnish as desired and serve with dippers of your choice.*

TIP
The thickness of this hummus will vary depending on the peas. Larger, starchier peas will require more liquid to become smooth.

VIENNESE ICED COFFEE

Makes 2 servings

Ingredients:

1 cup strong cold coffee
2 tablespoons chocolate syrup
1 cup half & half
2 scoops vanilla ice cream
2 cups ice cubes
Whipped cream, for topping
Coffee grounds, for topping (optional)

Method:

1. *Place all ingredients, except whipped cream and coffee grounds, into the Blender Jar; cover with Lid.*
2. *Blend on SPEED 9-10 until smooth (do not over blend or the iced coffee will get warm from the friction).*
3. *Pour into glasses then top with whipped cream and coffee grounds if desired before serving cold.*

BLUEBERRY PANCAKES

Makes 4 servings

Ingredients:

2 large eggs

1 cup all purpose flour

1 cup whole milk

3 tablespoons unsalted butter, melted and divided

1/2 teaspoon baking powder

1/2 teaspoon kosher salt

1 cup blueberries

Powdered sugar, for serving

Method:

1. *Place eggs, flour, milk, 2 tablespoons butter, baking powder and salt into the Blender Jar; cover with Lid.*
2. *Blend on SPEED 1-2 for 10 seconds or until smooth (use Tamper as needed).*
3. *Preheat half of the remaining butter in a nonstick skillet over medium-high heat.*
4. *Pour batter into the skillet, 1/4 cup for each pancake.*
5. *Scatter some blueberries over the pancakes then cook for 2-3 minutes or until bottoms are golden brown and bubbles form on top.*
6. *Flip pancakes over and cook for an additional 2-3 minutes or until golden brown.*
7. *Remove pancakes then repeat with remaining batter.*
8. *Serve blueberry-side up with additional blueberries and dusted with powdered sugar.*

TIP

Change this recipe into banana pancakes by pulsing a ripe banana into the batter and then topping finished pancakes with additional banana slices.

ALMOND
MILK

Makes 3 1/2 cups

Ingredients:

2 cups raw almonds, with the skin on
3 cups cold water
2-3 Medjool dates (optional)
1 teaspoon vanilla extract (optional)

Method:

1. *Soak almonds in the water for 2 hours at room temperature or soak in the refrigerator for up to 2 days.*

2. *Transfer the soaked almonds with the water to the Blender Jar then add remaining ingredients if desired; cover with Lid.*

3. *Blend using the SMOOTHIE PROGRAM twice (2 cycles).*

4. *When blending is complete, pour through a fine strainer or nut milk bag (leftover pulp can be added to smoothies if desired).*

5. *Store in the refrigerator for up to 5 days or freeze for up to 3 months.*

6. *Stir before use if milk separates into layers (this is normal).*

TIP
Use cashews or hazelnuts instead of almonds to make a different nut milk.

BAKED POTATO SOUP

Makes 4 servings

Ingredients:

2 cups chicken stock
3 small baked, leftover Russet potatoes, divided
2 tablespoons Parmesan cheese, grated
1/2 cup sharp Cheddar cheese + more for serving
Kosher salt and fresh pepper to taste
4 tablespoons sour cream
4 bacon strips, cooked and crumbled
1 green onion, sliced

Method:

1. *Place the stock, 2 potatoes, Parmesan cheese and 1/2 cup Cheddar cheese into the Blender Jar then season to taste with salt and pepper; cover with Lid.*
2. *Blend using the SOUP PROGRAM until hot and steamy.*
3. *When blending is complete, dice the remaining potato, add to the Blender Jar with the soup, cover with Lid and slowly PULSE until chunky or desired consistency is achieved.*
4. *Serve soup in bowls topped with additional Cheddar cheese, sour cream, bacon and green onions.*

BUTTERNUT SQUASH SOUP

Makes 4-6 servings

Ingredients:

2 tablespoons unsalted butter

1 small yellow onion, quartered

1 bag (14 ounces) frozen butternut squash, thawed

2 cups vegetable or chicken stock

Kosher salt and fresh pepper to taste

1 tablespoon honey

1 teaspoon apple cider vinegar

Cranberry relish, store-bought, for serving

Chives, sliced, for serving

Method:

1. *Place all ingredients, except relish and chives, into the Blender Jar; cover with Lid.*
2. *Blend using the SOUP PROGRAM until hot and steamy.*
3. *Serve in bowls topped with cranberry relish and chives.*

CAESAR SALAD DRESSING

Makes about 2 cups

Ingredients:

4 jarred or canned anchovy fillets
3 garlic cloves
2 large pasteurized eggs
1/4 cup fresh lemon juice
2 tablespoons red wine vinegar
1/2 teaspoon freshly ground black pepper
1/2 teaspoon kosher salt or to taste
1/2 teaspoon Worcestershire sauce
1 cup Parmesan cheese, grated
1 1/4 cups olive oil

Method:

1. *Place all ingredients, except olive oil, into the Blender Jar; cover with Lid.*
2. *Blend on SPEED 9-10 for 30 seconds or until smooth and creamy (use Tamper as needed).*
3. *While blending, pour the olive oil through the Lid opening in a thin stream and blend until smooth.*
4. *When blending is complete, transfer dressing to a lidded container.*
5. *Store in the refrigerator for up to 1 week.*

FRUIT BASED
BABY FOOD

Makes about 3/4 cup

Ingredients:

Peaches:
1 cup fresh peaches
1/4 cup water or organic fruit juice

Apples:
1 medium golden delicious apple, peeled and cored
1/4 cup water or organic fruit juice
(cut apples into quarters then steam until tender prior to blending)

Blueberries:
1 cup fresh blueberries
1/4 cup water or organic fruit juice

Plums:
4 plums, pits removed
1/4 cup water or organic fruit juice
(steam until soft prior to blending)

Method:

1. *Place desired fruits and water or juice into the Blender Jar; cover with Lid.*
2. *Blend on SPEED 9-10 until smooth, scraping down the Blender Jar as needed.*
3. *If desired, pour mixture through a fine mesh strainer for a smoother consistency.*
4. *Serve within 2 days or freeze in individual portions for later use.*

TIP

The easiest way to freeze individual portions of baby food is in silicone ice cube trays. Fill the trays to the top with baby food, cover, freeze then pop them out into a plastic zipper bag and store in the freezer until ready to use. The silicone makes for much easier removal since you can just turn it inside out.

EASIEST
HOLLANDAISE SAUCE

Makes about 1 1/2 cups

Ingredients:

1 cup unsalted butter, cut into chunks

6 large egg yolks

1/3 cup fresh lemon juice

1 teaspoon kosher salt or to taste

1/4 teaspoon cayenne pepper (optional)

1/4 teaspoon freshly ground white pepper (optional)

RECIPES

Method:

1. *Place all ingredients into the Blender Jar; cover with Lid.*
2. *Blend on SPEED 9-10 for 5-6 minutes while monitoring the temperature using an instant read thermometer through the Lid opening until temperature reaches 170°F (do not touch the blades with the thermometer).*
3. *When blending is complete, immediately transfer sauce into a serving vessel.*
4. *Serve hot.*

TIP

You can keep this sauce hot for up to 2 hours by pouring it into a warmed thermos. Sauce must stay hot or very warm or it will curdle.

EASY

Makes about 1 1/2 cups

Ingredients:

8 garlic cloves
4 cups fresh basil leaves, packed
1 cup spinach leaves (optional)
1 cup extra-virgin olive oil
1/4 cup pine nuts, lightly toasted
Kosher salt to taste
1 cup Parmesan cheese, shredded

Method:

1. *Place all ingredients, except cheese, into the Blender Jar; cover with Lid.*
2. *Blend on SPEED 9-10 for 30 seconds or until combined (use Tamper as needed).*
3. *Add the cheese to the blender and PULSE to combine.*
4. *Pour pesto into storage containers.*
5. *Keep refrigerated for up to 3 days or frozen for up to 3 months.*

TIP

Wolfgang suggests keeping
the cheese separate if planning
to use pesto for sautéing or
using with fish which does not
always go well with cheese.

Pesto 11/11

EASY CREPES

Makes 4 cups (about 24 crepes)

Ingredients:

5 large eggs

3 cups whole milk

2 tablespoons unsalted butter, melted

1 teaspoon kosher salt

1 tablespoon brandy (optional)

1 teaspoon vanilla extract

1 tablespoon sugar

2 cups unbleached all purpose flour

1 tablespoon canola oil + more for the skillet

Fillings and toppings, as desired

Method:

1. *Place all ingredients, except oil, fillings and toppings, in the order listed into the Blender Jar; cover with Lid.*
2. *Blend on SPEED 1-2 for 1 minute or until smooth.*
3. *Preheat a small amount of oil in a small skillet or crepe pan over medium heat; swirl to coat.*
4. *Pour 2 tablespoons crepe batter into the skillet and swirl to form a crepe. If there are holes, add some additional batter or pour out excess batter if needed.*
5. *Cook for 30 seconds or until edges look dry then lift the edge of the crepe using a small off-set spatula and flip over gently.*
6. *Cook other side for 10 seconds then invert skillet over a plate to release the crepe.*
7. *Add a small amount of oil to the skillet and repeat with remaining batter.*
8. *If stacking the crepes, place a piece of parchment paper between each crepe if desired.*
9. *Fill, garnish and serve as desired. Crepes can be covered and frozen for up to 1 month. The batter can be refrigerated for up to 3 days or frozen for up to 3 months.*

CHOCOLATE FONDUE

Makes 3 cups

Ingredients:

2 cups semi-sweet chocolate chips
1 1/4 cups heavy cream
3 tablespoons unsalted butter
1 teaspoon vanilla extract
1 teaspoon instant coffee granules (optional)
Assorted fruits and cookies, for dipping

Method:

1. *Place all ingredients, except fruits and cookies, into the Blender Jar; cover with Lid.*
2. *Blend using the SOUP PROGRAM until hot and steamy.*
3. *When blending is complete, pour into a serving dish and serve hot with fruits and cookies.*

TIP

For white chocolate fondue, omit the semi-sweet chocolate chips as well as the coffee granules, reduce cream to 1 cup then add 3 cups white chocolate chips.

NO FEAR BLENDER
CHEESE SOUFFLÉS

Makes 4 servings

Ingredients:

1/3 cup Parmesan cheese, grated

4 large eggs

1 cup shredded Swiss cheese + plus more for topping

1/2 cup cream cheese, softened

1/3 cup whole milk

A few shakes bottled hot sauce

1 tablespoon ketchup

1 teaspoon dry mustard powder

Kosher salt and fresh pepper to taste

Method:

1. *Preheat oven to 400°F.*
2. *Apply nonstick spray to 4 espresso cups or standard size straight-sided ramekins.*
3. *Sprinkle Parmesan cheese into a cup or ramekin and tilt all around to coat with cheese.*
4. *Repeat with remaining cups or ramekins then place them on a sheet pan; set aside.*
5. *Place remaining ingredients into the Blender Jar; cover with Lid.*
6. *Blend on SPEED 9-10 for 30 seconds or until smooth.*
7. *Divide mixture between the cups or ramekins then top with additional Swiss cheese.*
8. *Bake on center rack in the oven for 20-30 minutes or until well puffed and brown.*
9. *When baking is complete, remove and serve immediately before they deflate.*

MODERN NO LUMP GRAVY

Makes 2 cups

Ingredients:

1 1/2 cups beef or chicken stock

4 tablespoons unsalted butter

2 tablespoons yellow onions, chopped

4-5 Italian style bread slices

Kosher salt and fresh pepper to taste

Method:

1. Place all ingredients into the Blender Jar; cover with Lid.
2. Blend using the SOUP PROGRAM until hot and steamy.
3. When blending is complete, serve as desired.

HOMEMADE MAYONNAISE

Makes about 2 cups

Ingredients:

2 large pasteurized eggs
1 teaspoon fine sea salt
1 tablespoon dry mustard powder
1 tablespoon white vinegar
1 tablespoon fresh lemon juice
Pinch of white pepper (optional)
2 cups canola oil

Method:

1. *Place all ingredients, except oil, into the Blender Jar; cover with Lid.*
2. *Blend on SPEED 9-10 for a few seconds.*
3. *While blending, pour the oil through the Lid opening in a thin stream, not letting the oil pool on top of the mayonnaise.*
4. *Blend until mayonnaise has thickened then transfer to an airtight container.*
5. *Mayonnaise can be stored in the refrigerator for up to 1 week.*

TIP

For a pesto mayonnaise, add 1 cup loosely packed basil leaves, 3 garlic cloves and use olive oil instead of canola oil.

BEGINNER
GREEN SMOOTHIE

Makes 2 servings

Ingredients:

1 cup green grapes
1 very ripe banana
1 cup spinach leaves
1 kiwi, peeled
1 cup pineapple chunks
1 tangerine, mostly peeled
1 small carrot
1/2 cup plain yogurt
1 cup ice cubes

Method:

1. *Place all ingredients in the order listed into the Blender Jar; cover with Lid.*
2. *Blend using the SMOOTHIE PROGRAM.*
3. *When blending is complete, pour into glasses and serve.*

TIP

As a general rule, when blending smoothies containing fruits and vegetables, keep the ratio 60% fruit and 40% vegetables for a slightly sweet, balanced tasting smoothie.

PINEAPPLE COCONUT
SORBET

Makes 3-4 servings

Ingredients:

1 pound frozen pineapple chunks

1 cup coconut milk

1/2 cup powdered sugar or sweetener of your choice

1/2 cup toasted coconut

Method:

1. *Place all ingredients into the Blender Jar; cover with Lid and insert the Tamper.*

2. *Blend on SPEED 9-10, pushing the pineapple chunks towards the blades using the Tamper until mixture is smooth and thick. Do not over blend or melting will occur from the friction.*

3. *When blending is complete, serve immediately.*

PEACH COBBLER SMOOTHIE

Makes 2 servings

Ingredients:

1 bag (12 ounces) frozen peaches, thawed

1/2 teaspoon ground cinnamon

4 Medjool dates

1 cup vanilla yogurt

2 tablespoons peach jam

1 cup ice cubes

Method:

1. *Place all ingredients into the Blender Jar; cover with Lid.*
2. *Blend using the SMOOTHIE PROGRAM.*
3. *When blending is complete, pour into glasses, garnish as desired and serve.*

PEA SOUP

Makes 4 servings

Ingredients:

1 bag (12 ounces) frozen peas, thawed (reserve some peas for topping)
4 green onions
1 tablespoon kosher salt
1 3/4 cups chicken stock
2 teaspoons fresh lemon juice
2 teaspoons granulated sugar
2 tablespoons heavy cream
Sour cream, for garnishing

Method:

1. *Place all ingredients, except sour cream, into the Blender Jar; cover with Lid.*
2. *Blend using the SOUP PROGRAM until hot and steamy.*
3. *Pour into soup bowls then top with sour cream and reserved peas before serving.*

LEMON BUTTERMILK PIE

Makes one 9-inch pie

Ingredients:

2/3 cup granulated sugar

1/2 cup unsalted butter, melted

1/2 lemon, quartered

1/4 cup buttermilk

2/3 cup heavy cream

8 large egg yolks

1 teaspoon pure vanilla extract

1 store-bought 9-inch pie crust, unbaked

Powdered sugar, for serving

Method:

1. Preheat oven to 375°F.
2. Place the sugar, butter, lemon, buttermilk, cream, eggs and vanilla into the Blender Jar; cover with Lid.
3. PULSE until ingredients are frothy and lemon pieces are specks.
4. Pour mixture into a pie crust-lined pie pan.
5. Bake for 15 minutes then lower oven temperature to 300°F and bake for an additional 30-35 minutes or until just set (a paring knife inserted off-center should come out clean).
6. When baking is complete, remove and serve at room temperature dusted with powdered sugar.

TIP

You can prepare the batter for this recipe a few days ahead of time and refrigerate it then bake the pie the day you plan on serving it for the best taste and texture.

BANANA PEANUT BUTTER ICE CREAM

Makes 2-3 servings

Ingredients:

1 cup almond milk

2-3 Medjool dates

1/2 teaspoon vanilla extract

3 tablespoons peanut butter (or use the Homemade Peanut Butter on page 17)

4 very ripe frozen bananas, cut into thirds

Method:

1. *Place almond milk and dates into the Blender Jar; cover with Lid.*
2. *Blend on SPEED 9-10 for 15 seconds then scrape down the Blender Jar.*
3. *Replace Lid and blend for an additional 5 seconds then scrape again.*
4. *Add remaining ingredients to the Blender Jar; cover with Lid.*
5. *Blend on SPEED 9-10, pushing the bananas towards the blades using the Tamper until mixture is smooth and thick. Do not over blend or melting will occur from the friction.*
6. *When blending is complete, serve immediately.*

TIP

Don't mix for too long or you will be having a milkshake instead of ice cream. You can add chocolate chips to this as well if desired.

ORANGE CREAMSICLE POPS

Makes about 6 pops

Ingredients:

1/3 cup whole milk
4 scoops vanilla ice cream
Zest from 1 orange
1 cup fresh orange juice
1 teaspoon vanilla extract
1/4 teaspoon orange extract (optional)
1-2 drops orange food coloring (optional)

Method:

1. *Place all ingredients into the Blender Jar; cover with Lid.*
2. *Blend on SPEED 9-10 for 10 seconds or until creamy and smooth (use Tamper as needed).*
3. *Pour mixture into small paper cups or Popsicle molds.*
4. *Freeze for 1 hour or until fairly firm.*
5. *Insert Popsicle sticks into the center of each pop.*
6. *Freeze until solid before serving.*

PEANUT DIPPING SAUCE

Makes about 1 1/2 cups

Ingredients:

1 cup coconut milk + more if needed

2 garlic cloves

2/3 cup peanut butter

Zest and juice from 1 lime

1/4 cup granulated sugar

Soy sauce to taste

1 teaspoon dark sesame oil

1 tablespoon bottled fish sauce

Method:

1. *Place all ingredients into the Blender Jar; cover with Lid.*
2. *Blend on SPEED 9-10 for 20-30 seconds or until smooth. If mixture is too thick, add additional coconut milk until desired consistency is achieved.*
3. *When blending is complete, pour into a serving dish.*
4. *Sauce will keep in the refrigerator for up to 1 week.*

TIP

Try this sauce anywhere you would normally use Ranch dressing. If you have a peanut allergy try toasted cashews or hazelnuts instead of the peanuts.

BANANA BREAD

Makes 1 loaf

Ingredients:

4 large overripe bananas
1/2 cup unsalted butter
2 large eggs
1 cup sugar
1/2 teaspoon vanilla extract
1/2 teaspoon kosher salt
2 tablespoons sour cream
1 teaspoon baking soda
1/2 teaspoon baking powder
2 cups all purpose flour
1/2 cup walnuts

Method:

1. *Preheat oven to 350°F and butter a large loaf pan; set aside.*
2. *Place the banana, butter, eggs, sugar, vanilla, salt and sour cream into the Blender Jar; cover with Lid.*
3. *Blend on SPEED 5-6 until butter pieces are small and mixture looks curdled.*
4. *Add remaining ingredients, except walnuts, to the Blender Jar; cover with Lid then blend on SPEED 1-2 for 3 seconds.*
5. *Add the walnuts through the Lid opening and PULSE for 1-2 seconds.*
6. *Scrape down the Blender Jar then blend again for 3 seconds or until just combined.*
7. *Transfer mixture to the loaf pan and smooth the top.*
8. *Bake for 45-55 minutes or until domed, cracked down the center and well browned.*
9. *When baking is complete, serve warm or at room temperature.*

SWEET CORN CHOWDER

Makes 4 servings

Ingredients:

2 tablespoons unsalted butter
Kosher salt and fresh pepper to taste
1 1/2 cups chicken stock
1/3 cup half & half
2 cups frozen yellow corn kernels, thawed and divided + more for garnish
1 teaspoon fresh lemon juice
3 green onions

Method:

1. *Place all ingredients, except 1 cup of corn, into the Blender Jar; cover with Lid.*
2. *Blend using the SOUP PROGRAM until hot and steamy.*
3. *Add remaining 1 cup of corn and briefly blend on SPEED 1-2 just to break up the corn or until desired consistency.*
4. *Ladle into bowls, top with additional corn, garnish as desired and serve hot.*

CURRIED SWEET POTATO SOUP

Makes 4 servings

Ingredients:

1 small yellow onion, quartered

2 small sweet potatoes, roasted

2 fresh ginger coins

2 garlic cloves

Crushed red pepper flakes to taste

1/2 cup coconut milk

Zest and juice from 1/2 lime

2 tablespoons curry powder or garam masala

1 tablespoon honey

Kosher salt and fresh pepper to taste

1 1/2 cups vegetable stock

A handful of cilantro + more for serving

Method:

1. *Place all ingredients, except cilantro for serving, into the Blender Jar; cover with Lid.*
2. *Blend using the SOUP PROGRAM until hot and steamy.*
3. *When blending is complete, ladle into bowls, top with cilantro, garnish as desired and serve.*

BLENDER
COLESLAW

Makes 8 servings

Ingredients:

2 carrots, peeled and roughly cut

1/2 small head green cabbage, cut into chunks

1/4 head purple cabbage, cut into chunks

1 tart apple, cored and roughly cut

Water as needed

1 cup mayonnaise

2 tablespoons cider vinegar

1/3 cup granulated sugar

2 tablespoons yellow mustard

Kosher salt and fresh pepper to taste

Method:

1. *Fill Blender Jar half full of carrots, cabbage and apples.*
2. *Add water until Blender Jar is half full; cover with Lid.*
3. *Blend on SPEED 1-2 for 2-5 seconds or until finely chopped.*
4. *Pour blender contents through a fine mesh strainer.*
5. *Repeat until all vegetables are chopped.*
6. *Squeeze as much water as possible from the strained mixture then transfer to a large bowl.*
7. *Place remaining ingredients into the Blender Jar; cover with Lid.*
8. *Blend on SPEED 1-2 for 5-10 seconds or until combined.*
9. *Pour mayonnaise mixture over the bowl contents and mix well.*
10. *Cover and refrigerate for a minimum of 1 hour before serving.*
11. *Coleslaw will keep in the refrigerator for up to 3 days.*

TIP

The water used in this recipe is just to facilitate proper chopping of the vegetables so be sure to squeeze out all excess water after blending to prevent the flavor of this dressing to get watered down. You can add other vegetables to this recipe as well to make different variations such as broccoli stems, pineapple or bell peppers.

FROZEN BRAZILIAN LIMEADE

Makes 2 servings

Ingredients:

Zest and juice from 6 limes

2/3 cup water

1/2 cup sweetened condensed milk

4 cups ice cubes

3 ounces cachaça or rum (optional)

Method:

1. *Place all ingredients into the Blender Jar; cover with Lid.*
2. *Blend on SPEED 9-10 for 20 seconds or until smooth.*
3. *When blending is complete, pour into glasses, garnish as desired and serve.*

MELON & CUCUMBER REFRESHER

Makes 4 cups

Ingredients:

1 cup green grapes

1 honeydew melon wedge

1 piece cucumber (about 1 cup)

1 teaspoon lime zest

Juice from 1/2 lime

A few fresh mint leaves

1 cup ice cubes

Method:

1. *Place all ingredients into the Blender Jar; cover with Lid.*
2. *Blend on SPEED 9-10 until smooth.*
3. *Pour into glasses, garnish as desired and serve.*

ROASTED CAULIFLOWER
HUMMUS

Makes 3 cups

Ingredients:

1 head cauliflower
6 whole garlic cloves
1 medium yellow onion, cut into wedges
1 lemon, unpeeled and quartered
2 tablespoons unsalted butter, melted
Kosher salt and fresh pepper to taste
2 tablespoons olive oil
1/2 teaspoon fresh thyme leaves

Method:

1. Preheat oven to 400°F.
2. Cut cauliflower into florets then transfer to a sheet pan.
3. Scatter garlic, onions and lemon around the cauliflower then drizzle with the butter.
4. Season with salt and pepper then roast in the oven for 25 minutes or until deeply caramelized.
5. When roasting is complete, transfer pan contents, except lemons, to the Blender Jar.
6. Squeeze the juice from the roasted lemon pieces into the Blender Jar and add 1 whole roasted lemon piece to the Blender Jar.
7. Add remaining ingredients and cover with Lid.
8. Blend on SPEED 9-10 for 20 seconds or until smooth.
9. When blending is complete, garnish as desired and serve.

PIÑA COLADA

Makes 2 servings

Ingredients:

2 fresh pineapple wedges
1/2 cup canned coconut cream
Zest and juice from 1 lime
2 ounces white rum
2 cups ice cubes

Method:

1. Place all ingredients into the Blender Jar; cover with Lid.
2. Blend on SPEED 9-10 until smooth.
3. When blending is complete, pour into glasses, garnish as desired and serve.

APPLE PIE SMOOTHIE

Makes 2 servings

Ingredients:

1 apple, quartered
2 Medjool dates
1/4 cup apple juice concentrate
1/2 teaspoon apple pie spice
1/3 cup vanilla yogurt
1 cup ice cubes

Method:

1. *Place all ingredients into the Blender Jar; cover with Lid and insert Tamper.*
2. *Blend using the SMOOTHIE PROGRAM (use Tamper as needed).*
3. *When blending is complete, pour into glasses and serve.*

HOMEMADE CHOCOLATE HAZELNUT SPREAD

Makes 2 cups

Ingredients:

2 cups hazelnuts, skins left on
1/2 cup coconut oil
1/2 cup cocoa powder
1 cup powdered sugar
1 tablespoon vanilla extract
Pinch of kosher salt

Method:

1. *Preheat oven to 350°F. Spread nuts in a single layer on a sheet pan and bake for 15-20 minutes or until brown and fragrant; remove and let cool.*
2. *Place nuts and remaining ingredients into the Blender Jar; cover with Lid and insert Tamper.*
3. *Blend on SPEED 9-10, pushing the nuts towards the blades using the Tamper.*
4. *Blend for 1-3 minutes or until desired consistency is achieved.*
5. *Keep covered at room temperature for up to 1 week.*

CHOCOLATE GRASSHOPPER TARTS

Makes two 6-inch tarts

Ingredients:

For the Crust:

30 chocolate wafers

6 tablespoons unsalted butter, melted

For the Filling:

1 1/2 cups heavy cream

1/2 teaspoon vanilla extract

3 tablespoons powdered sugar

1/4 cup crème de menthe liqueur

1/3 cup white chocolate chips, melted

Method:

1. Place the wafers into the Blender Jar; cover with Lid.
2. PULSE until fine crumbs are achieved then transfer to a mixing bowl.
3. Stir butter into crumbs until combined then transfer to two tart pans.
4. Press crust evenly into bottom and sides of the pans then set aside.
5. Rinse Blender Jar with cold water then add the cream, vanilla and sugar; cover with Lid.
6. PULSE until cream thickens but does not become too stiff.
7. Remove to a mixing bowl then fold in remaining filling ingredients until smooth.
8. Scrape mixture into the crumb-lined tart pans.
9. Chill for 1 hour or up to 4 hours then garnish as desired and serve cold.

TIP

The blender is the perfect kitchen tool for this recipe because it has the ability to achieve a silky smooth filling. You can prepare the filling up to 3 days in advance and refrigerate it. Don't fill the tarts until the day you want to serve them so that the crust stays crunchy. If you really love chocolate, add a tablespoon of melted chocolate to the bottom of the tart shells before topping with the grasshopper filling.

RECIPES

YORKSHIRE PUDDING

Makes one 8-inch pudding

Ingredients:

1 cup whole milk

5 large eggs

1 cup all purpose flour

1 tablespoon powdered sugar

1 tablespoon kosher salt or to taste

1/4 cup Parmesan cheese, grated

Pinch of cayenne pepper or bottled hot sauce

1/4 cup vegetable oil (neutral in flavor)

Method:

1. *Preheat an 8x8-inch pan in the oven at 450°F.*
2. *Place all ingredients, except oil, into the Blender Jar; cover with Lid.*
3. *Blend on SPEED 10 for 20 seconds.*
4. *Using potholders, pour the oil into the preheated pan, tilting pan to coat the bottom and halfway up the sides.*
5. *Place in oven then pour batter into the center of the hot pan (it should sizzle).*
6. *Bake for 20-30 minutes or until dramatically puffed and brown (do not open oven until done).*
7. *Remove and serve immediately with a roast or as desired (Yorkshire pudding will deflate quickly).*

ZUCCHINI NUT BLENDER MUFFINS

Makes 6 servings

Ingredients:

1/3 cup pecans
2 cups zucchini, chopped
1/2 cup unsalted butter, melted
1/4 cup rolled oats
2 large eggs
1/2 teaspoon vanilla extract
1/2 teaspoon kosher salt
1 1/2 teaspoons baking soda
1/4 cup milk
1 1/4 cups all purpose flour

Method:

1. Preheat oven to 375°F. Spread pecans in a single layer on a sheet pan and bake for 15-20 minutes or until brown and fragrant; remove and let cool.
2. Grease a large 6-spot muffin tin.
3. Place all ingredients, except pecans, into the Blender Jar; cover with Lid.
4. Blend on SPEED 3-4 for 8-10 seconds or until smooth.
5. Scrape down the Blender Jar, add the pecans then cover with Lid.
6. Blend on SPEED 1-2 just to break up the pecans a bit.
7. Divide mixture between muffin tin wells, filling each until 3/4 full.
8. Bake at 375°F for 20-25 minutes or until well browned and domed.
9. When baking is complete, remove, garnish as desired and serve hot.

TIP

If your muffin tin is smaller, repeat with remaining batter to make another batch or keep batter refrigerated for up to 3 days for later use.

ENTIRE LEMON
LEMONADE

Makes 1 quart

Ingredients:

4 lemons, unpeeled and halved

1/2 to 2/3 cup granulated sugar or sugar substitute

3 cups ice cubes

3 cups cold water

Club soda, for serving

Method:

1. *Place all ingredients, except club soda, into the Blender Jar; cover with Lid and insert Tamper.*
2. *Blend on SPEED 9-10, using the Tamper if needed until no chunks of lemon remain.*
3. *Strain lemonade to remove pulp bits.*
4. *Add more ice cubes and club soda until desired sweetness is achieved.*
5. *Serve immediately.*

TIP

For a variation, try using limes instead of lemons but strain the lemonade right away as the lime rind and pith are considerably more bitter. You can also use tangerines but you will need to decrease the sugar since tangerines are naturally sweeter fruit.

NO CHURN CHOCOLATE
ICE CREAM

Makes 4 servings

Ingredients:

2 cups heavy cream
1 can (14 ounces) sweetened condensed milk
1 teaspoon vanilla extract
1/4 cup dark cocoa powder
Sprinkles, for serving

Method:

1. *Place the cream into the Blender Jar; cover with Lid.*
2. *Blend on SPEED 5-6 for 15 seconds or until thickened (do not over blend).*
3. *Add remaining ingredients, except sprinkles, then cover with Lid and blend on SPEED 1-2 just to incorporate.*
4. *Scrape mixture into a storage container and cover.*
5. *Freeze for a minimum of 4 hours or up to 2 days.*
6. *Top with sprinkles and serve as desired.*

TIP

Turn this into a chocolate salted caramel ice cream by layering store-bought caramel sauce, chocolate fudge sauce and a sprinkle of sea salt into the storage container.

SWEET COOKIE
BUTTER

Makes 2 cups

Ingredients:

2 cups chocolate sandwich double crème filled cookies

1/2 cup unsalted butter, softened

Pinch of kosher salt

1 teaspoon vanilla extract

1/4 cup heavy cream

Pretzel rods, for dipping

Method:

1. *Place all ingredients, except pretzel rods, into the Blender Jar; cover with Lid and insert Tamper.*
2. *Blend on SPEED 9-10, pushing the cookies towards the blades using the Tamper; scrape down the sides of the Blender Jar as needed.*
3. *Blend until smooth then transfer butter into a serving dish.*
4. *Butter will keep in the refrigerator for up to 1 week.*
5. *Soften in the microwave before use if desired then serve with pretzel rods for dipping.*

TIP

You can substitute your favorite cookies for the sandwich cookies in this recipe. If they are not crème filled, simply add more butter. I love coconut cookies and use coconut oil in place of the butter.

BUFFALO CHICKEN
DIP

Makes 3 cups

Ingredients:

1 package (8 ounces) cream cheese, softened

1/2 cup mayonnaise

1/3 cup sour cream

1/3 cup bottled wing sauce + more for serving

Kosher salt and fresh pepper to taste

1 cup cooked leftover chicken

1/2 cup blue cheese crumbles, for topping

Crackers and celery sticks, for serving

Method:

1. *Place the cream cheese, mayonnaise, sour cream and 1/3 cup wing sauce into the Blender Jar; season to taste with salt and pepper then cover with Lid.*
2. *Blend using the SOUP PROGRAM until hot and steamy.*
3. *When blending is complete, add the chicken, cover with Lid and blend on SPEED 1 to break up the chicken until chunky.*
4. *Pour dip into a serving dish and top with blue cheese crumbles.*
5. *Drizzle with additional wing sauce then serve with crackers and celery.*

GREEN GODDESS DRESSING

Makes about 1 1/2 cups

Ingredients:

2 garlic cloves
1 packed cup of a mixture of tarragon leaves, parsley, basil leaves and spinach leaves
1 large pasteurized egg
1/4 cup apple cider vinegar
2 jarred or canned anchovy fillets (about 1 teaspoon)
1 tablespoon capers
1 tablespoon granulated sugar
Kosher salt and fresh pepper to taste
1 1/4 cups canola oil

Method:

1. *Place all ingredients, except oil, into the Blender Jar; cover with Lid and insert Tamper.*
2. *Blend on SPEED 1-2 until fairly smooth (use Tamper as needed).*
3. *Remove Tamper then blend on SPEED 9-10.*
4. *While blending, pour the oil through the Lid opening in a thin stream, not letting the oil pool on top of the dressing.*
5. *Blend for an additional 30 seconds, scraping down the Blender Jar sides if necessary.*
6. *Taste carefully and adjust seasoning by adding more sugar and salt if desired.*
7. *Serve over your favorite salad or use as a dip.*

BLACKBERRY SORBET

Makes 3-4 servings

Ingredients:

1 pound frozen blackberries

1 cup powdered sugar or sweetener of your choice

1 cup grape juice

Method:

1. Place all ingredients into the Blender Jar; cover with Lid and insert the Tamper.
2. Blend on SPEED 9-10, pushing the blackberries towards the blades using the Tamper until mixture is smooth and thick. Do not over blend or melting will occur from the friction.
3. When blending is complete, serve immediately.

STRAWBERRY SHAKE

Makes 2 servings

Ingredients:

1/2 pound fresh strawberries, hulled and sliced
2 tablespoons granulated sugar
1 teaspoon vanilla extract
4 scoops vanilla ice cream (or use the No Churn Ice Cream on page 18)
1/2 cup whole milk
Whipped cream, for serving

Method:

1. *Place all ingredients, except whipped cream, into the Blender Jar; cover with Lid.*
2. *Blend on SPEED 9-10 for 20 seconds or until smooth (use Tamper as needed).*
3. *Pour into glasses, top with whipped cream and serve.*

VEGAN "CHEESE" SAUCE

Makes about 2 cups

Ingredients:

1 cup water
1/4 medium yellow onion, chopped
1 medium carrot, chopped
1 medium Russet potato, chopped (about 1 cup)
4 tablespoons coconut oil or vegan margarine
2 tablespoons light miso paste
1 tablespoon sun-dried tomatoes
1/2 teaspoon paprika
2/3 cup cashews, raw
1 tablespoon store-bought Dijon mustard
1 tablespoon fresh lemon juice
Kosher salt and fresh pepper to taste

Method:

1. *Combine the water, onions, carrots and potatoes in a small pot.*
2. *Bring to a simmer then cook for 10 minutes or until soft.*
3. *Transfer pot contents to the Blender Jar, add remaining ingredients then cover with Lid.*
4. *Blend using the SOUP PROGRAM until hot and steamy.*
5. *When blending is complete, serve as desired.*
6. *Keep refrigerated for up to 1 week.*

TIP

Boiling the vegetables first is important as it changes the starch in them and makes for an incredibly silky, thick sauce.

RASPBERRY COULIS

Makes 1 3/4 cups

Ingredients:

1 package (12 ounces) frozen raspberries, thawed
1/2 cup granulated sugar

Method:

1. *Place all ingredients into the Blender Jar; cover with Lid.*
2. *Blend on SPEED 9-10 for 20 seconds.*
3. *Transfer to a serving vessel and use as desired.*
4. *Keep refrigerated for up to 1 week.*

TIP

If you want a very thick raspberry sauce, blend for about 30 seconds on SPEED 9-10. This breaks up the seeds completely and releases more of the pectin they contain. Pectin is what makes jams and sauces get thick. Also, use this same formula to make sauces using other fruits (adjust sugar if other fruits are naturally less tart). If you need to avoid sugar, add 1/4 cup water and your favorite sweetener to taste. The color will be lighter but it will still taste great.

BLENDER VANILLA CUSTARD SAUCE

Makes 2 1/2 cups

Ingredients:

6 large egg yolks
2 cups half & half
Seeds from 1/3 of a vanilla bean or 1 tablespoon vanilla extract
1/3 cup granulated sugar
Pinch of kosher salt

Method:

1. *Place all ingredients into the Blender Jar; cover with Lid.*
2. *Blend on SPEED 9-10 for 3 minutes.*
3. *Continue to blend while monitoring the temperature using an instant read thermometer through the Lid opening until temperature reaches 170°F (do not touch the blades with the thermometer).*
4. *When temperature is reached, immediately pour the sauce into a bowl and whisk gently to slightly cool.*
5. *Serve as desired.*

BLENDER KALE
SALAD

Makes 4 servings

Ingredients:

1 large bunch kale
Water as needed
1/4 cup red wine vinegar
1 tablespoon dry mustard powder
2 tablespoons honey
1 garlic clove
2 tablespoons soy sauce or to taste
1 tablespoon light miso paste, optional (found in most health food stores)
1 cup hazelnut or olive oil
1/2 cup dark raisins
1/4 cup red onions, shaved
1/2 cup grapes
1/3 cup toasted hazelnuts
1/2 cup cherry tomatoes
1/4 cup blue cheese, crumbled

Method:

1. *Divide kale into 3 bunches, cutting kale in half if taller than Blender Jar.*
2. *Fill Blender Jar half full of water then add one bunch of kale; cover with Lid.*
3. *PULSE 3-5 times just until kale pieces are small; do not over blend.*
4. *Pour into a strainer (reserve the light green water for soups or smoothies if desired).*
5. *Press down hard to remove excess water then transfer to a bowl.*
6. *Repeat with remaining kale then set aside.*
7. *Place the vinegar, dry mustard, honey, garlic, soy and miso into the Blender Jar; cover with Lid.*
8. *Blend on SPEED 9-10 for 10 seconds.*
9. *Reduce blender to SPEED 5-6 then pour the olive oil through the Lid opening in a thin stream and blend for 10 seconds or until thick and emulsified.*
10. *Pour a small amount of dressing over the kale.*
11. *Add the raisins, onions, grapes, hazelnuts, tomatoes and blue cheese then toss gently, adding more dressing if needed.*
12. *Serve as desired.*
13. *Keep dressing refrigerated for up to 1 week.*

EDAMAME HUMMUS

Makes 2 cups

Ingredients:

1 bag (12 ounces) frozen and shelled edamame, thawed
2 garlic cloves
2 teaspoons curry powder
1 teaspoon dry ginger
1/3 cup coconut or olive oil
1/3 cup coconut or regular milk + more if needed
Zest and juice from 2 limes
1 tablespoon light miso paste
Kosher salt and fresh pepper to taste
Black sesame seeds, for serving
Dippers of your choice

Method:

1. *Place all ingredients, except sesame seeds and dippers, into the Blender Jar; cover with Lid.*
2. *Blend on SPEED 9-10 for 30 seconds.*
3. *Scrape down the Blender Jar, add more milk if necessary then cover with Lid and blend for an additional 10 seconds or until smooth.*
4. *Transfer to a serving container, top with black sesame seeds then serve with dippers of your choice.*

GOOEY BEER CHEDDAR DIP

Makes 4 servings

Ingredients:

1 can (12 ounces) beer, such as a Lager
3 Italian style bread slices
2 tablespoons unsalted butter
4 ounces extra-sharp Cheddar cheese, cubed
3 ounces mozzarella cheese, cubed
2 ounces Parmesan cheese, cubed
1 garlic clove
1 teaspoon paprika
Kosher salt and fresh pepper to taste
French bread or other dippers

Method:

1. *Place all ingredients, except dippers, into the Blender Jar; cover with Lid.*
2. *Blend using the SOUP PROGRAM until hot and steamy.*
3. *When blending is complete, pour into a bowl, garnish as desired and serve with French bread or other dippers.*

MALTED MILK
CHEESECAKE

Makes one 8-inch cheesecake

Ingredients:

3 packages (8 ounces each) cream cheese, softened

1/3 cup granulated sugar

5 large eggs

1/2 cup malted milk powder

1 store-bought 8-inch chocolate cookie pie crust

Malted milk balls, for topping and serving

Method:

1. *Preheat oven to 350°F.*
2. *Place the cream cheese, sugar, eggs and milk powder into the Blender Jar; cover with Lid.*
3. *Blend on SPEED 9-10 for 10 seconds to combine then transfer to the pie crust.*
4. *Scatter some malted milk balls over the cheesecake surface.*
5. *Bake for 30-35 minutes or until puffed and browned.*
6. *When baking is complete, remove and serve hot or warm with additional malted milk balls.*

PINEAPPLE
MARGARITA

Makes 2 servings

Ingredients:

2 fresh pineapple wedges

2 tablespoons sugar or agave syrup

Zest and juice from 2-3 limes + more for salt garnish

2 ounces tequila

1 ounce triple sec or orange liqueur

3 cups ice cubes

Kosher salt for rims of glass

Method:

1. *Place all ingredients, except salt, into the Blender Jar; cover with Lid.*
2. *Blend on SPEED 9-10 for 8 seconds or until smooth.*
3. *Use a piece of lime to moisten the rims of the glasses.*
4. *Dip glass rims in salt until rims are covered.*
5. *Pour margarita into glasses below the salt rim.*
6. *Garnish as desired and serve immediately.*

LEMON CURD

Makes 2 cups

Ingredients:

3 large egg yolks
2 large eggs
Zest from 2 lemons
1/3 cup fresh lemon juice
1/2 cup granulated sugar
2 sticks (1 cup) cold butter, chunked

Method:

1. *Place all ingredients into the Blender Jar; cover with Lid and insert Tamper.*
2. *Blend using the SOUP PROGRAM, pushing the butter onto the blades using the Tamper (mixture will appear curdled for a few seconds).*
3. *After blending for 4 minutes, monitor the temperature using an instant read thermometer through the Lid opening until temperature reaches 180°F (do not touch the blades with the thermometer) then transfer to a storage container.*
4. *Let cool for 30 minutes then refrigerate.*
5. *Keep refrigerated for up to 1 week or frozen for up to 3 months.*

INDEX

INDEX

FOR ALL OF MARIAN GETZ'S
COOKBOOKS AS WELL AS
COOKWARE, APPLIANCES, CUTLERY
AND KITCHEN ACCESSORIES
BY WOLFGANG PUCK

PLEASE VISIT
HSN.COM
(KEYWORD: WOLFGANG PUCK)